Dedication

This book is dedicated to
three exceptional martial arts teachers:

Professor Remy Amador Presas

Professor Wally Jay

and

Grandmaster Bram Frank

Domo arigato gozaimashita.

武士道

The Firearm as a Martial Arts Weapon

A book by
Michael W. Weissberg

Edited By
Linda R. Weissberg

WHITE MOUNTAIN PUBLISHING CO.

MIAMI, FLORIDA

2011

WM

WHITE MOUNTAIN PUBLISHING CO.
MIAMI, FLORIDA

Copyright 2011 by Michael W. Weissberg

First edition, second printing

Library of Congress Cataloging-in-Publication Data

Weissberg, Michael.

    The Firearm as a Martial Arts Weapon by Michael Weissberg – 1st ed.

Library of Congress Control Number (LCCN): **PCN** 2011933408

ISBN-10 0983486654
ISBN-13 9780983486657

11 10 9 8 7 6 5 4 3 2

Book design by Michael Weissberg
Printed in the United States of America

Also by
Michael W. Weissberg:

Honor, Glory, Respect:
Conducting Police Funerals

Processing Environmental Crime Scenes

What Every Cop Must Know:
Tactical Preparation for the Worst Day of Your
Life

Coming Soon
from
White Mountain
Publishing Company:

Off Duty: Concealed Weapons
Carry For Cops

Acknowledgements

Hajime ni.

I have been honored to become acquainted with the famous translator and author William Scott Wilson. Wilson is the most important author of Medieval Japanese literature in the world, bar none. Wilson translated The *Tao Te Ching, Hagakure, Go Rin No Sho, The Life-Giving Sword*, and *The Unfettered Mind*, in addition to authoring *The Lone Samurai,* and translating *Taiko* by Eiji Yoshikawa, the greatest Japanese writer of the modern age.

To have co-authored with Miyamoto Musashi, Takuan Sōhō, Yagyū Munenori, Yamamoto Tsunetomo, Lao Tzu, and Eiji Yoshikawa, would be like writing with Chaucer, Shakespeare, Marlowe, John Donne, Shelley, and Walter Raleigh.

I cannot even begin to understand how William Wilson even lives – I would have died from fright, pride, or both, to be associated with the greatest Asian writers of all time, who might arguably be the greatest writers of all time.

Wilson has invited me into his home, graced me with his knowledge, and allowed me to learn from him. I am supremely honored and truly humbled that he has read and commented on this book. I thank "Bill" for allowing me into his presence.

The genesis of this topic came from martial arts teacher and pistol instructor Ed Gottlieb. Ed originally wished to author a book about pistolcraft as a martial art. I took this idea and modified it into "the firearm as a martial arts weapon" and desired to include the long gun, taking Ed's idea and changing it.

I helped Ed to refine his idea to allow him to focus on the pistol, his favored weapon, and to figure out that his desire was more to write a book on pistolcraft than to create a marital science tome.

Ed's concept allowed me to explore my three favorite interests, firearms, martial arts, and the medieval period in Japan, in philosophy, history, art, poetry, ceramics, calligraphy, *Cha-no-yu*, and aesthetics. The genesis may belong to Ed, but this truly became my personal *bubishi. Bubishi* (武備志) is the Japanese pronunciation of the Chinese *wubei zhi*, "an account of military arts and science".

And of course, I thank my mother, who is also my favorite editor, who has been reading my writing for some thirty-five years. If there are any errors in this book, they are mine, not hers. Erika; thank you for being my wife.

About the Author:
Michael W. Weissberg

Michael Weissberg began his career as an educator in 1988. A graduate of the University of Miami, Weissberg holds Master's degrees from Nova Southeastern University, Florida International University, and Northcentral University.

A lifelong martial student, Weissberg was awarded his first black belt by Grandmaster Bram Frank; the belt was affirmed by Professors Remy Presas, Wally Jay, and George Dillman. Weissberg was subsequently promoted by Grandmaster Frank who acknowledges him as a personal student, and has granted him a school license.

Weissberg also acknowledges as his teachers Grandmaster Eddie Pagan (deceased), Grandmaster Graciela Casillas-Tortorelli, Grandmaster Joe Robaina, Grandmaster Ed Lake, Master John Ralston, and Master Tony Torre.

Ah, summer grasses!

All that remains

Of the warrior's dreams.

Matsuo Basho
松尾芭蕉

Firearms and Martial Arts: A Historical Perspective

A martial art is a series of bio mechanical movements designed to accomplish a set goal in the most effective and efficient way possible using the least amount of time, motion and energy to accomplish the task. The martial art delivers the most amount of energy to the desired result while expending the least amount of energy to do it.

Some suggest that any action, motion or task can be raised to the level of a martial art; throwing a baseball, eating soup, dancing, hammering a nail, or presenting a firearm from a pocket or a holster, can all be viewed as something that can be perfected.

The historical context for this is the liege lord who mandated that his *samurai* (Japanese for *"to serve"*) learn flower arranging, poetry composing, and *cha-no-yu*, the tea ceremony.

The *samurai* loved the poetry game, whereby a challenger would come up with the first line of a poem, a player would compose a poem with that first line being the initial line. The challenger would twist the poem, and make another from that one, usually with an ironic twist, which may have lightly belittled the other player.   The game was clever, and a master might win favor and prizes from the lord, who was normally the challenger. This game was a martial art itself; and woe be to the man who lost on purpose to curry favor.

One might say that if you can raise the efficiency of doing something you have lifted that particular action to a martial art. So if it takes for example six motions to sip soup, and you figure out how to sip soup in only 5 or 4 motions, you have lifted sipping soup to a quicker more efficient level; to the level of a martial art.

Efficiency is not the only tenet of a martial art; the activity must contain grace and audacity. Shimmen Miyamoto Musashi Masana, the *kensei* (sword saint) of medieval Japan, saw this grace and audacity in *Noh* acting, dance, calligraphy, ink drawing, flower arranging, pottery, and other arts that were unrelated to weaponry.

Musashi is reported to have noticed the cut of a peony stem made by swordsman Yagyū Sekishusai Muneyoshi, and the marks of the spatula on a plain tea bowl made by potter and swordsman Hon'ami Koetsu. The sudden best work of a master calligrapher, the masterwork of a plain tea bowl, and the ability to make a perfect cut when arranging flowers, are all simple things; they are simple things that take a lifetime to perfect.

Kata are the specific series of movements required to do something, and these specific movements take on a special perfection all their own. These movements have a life of their own and they can have a beautiful and very powerful use and function. *Kata* is usually a set of calisthenics used by martial artists to warm up and achieve muscle memory.

When a set of movements are proved to be the most efficient means of accomplishing a goal, they become like music, like an art form in their own right. They become beautiful and represent a harmony of unified motion to the practitioner who masters those movements. When this happens, it is said that we have "*kata*"; a very special, harmonious and powerful set of movements that can be performed and appreciated not only for their beauty and harmony of form and function, but also for the powerful results they produce.

The late 1500's were a special time. The Spanish were assembling their armada; the Jesuits were making significant inroads into China, Korea, and Japan; Shakespeare and Ben Johnson were performing their plays for the English; Musashi was active in formulating what would ultimately become the *Go Rin No Sho;* Tokugawa Iyeyasu, the shogun who united Japan, was preparing for his greatest battle, the battle of Battle of Sekigahara astride the Tōkaidō Road.

The Japanese used many weapons for both practice and warfare. The axe, the staff, the spear, the sword, the chain-ball-sickle (*kusarigama*), the arrow, and other edged weapons were all used on the battle field, but a new weapon was becoming slowly accepted: the matchlock musket.

A weakness of the matchlock was the necessity of keeping the match lit; if the match was not lit when the gun needed to be fired, the mechanism was useless, and the gun was useful only as a club. A socket type bayonet could be attached for attacks, but was much less effective against the sword.

In wet weather, damp match cord was hard to light and keep burning. At night, the match would glow in the darkness, revealing the gunner's location. The smell of burning matchcord, which was sometimes soaked in wine and saltpeter (potassium nitrate) was another way to identify a gunner.

The primary problem liege lords had with guns was the fact that honor and valor could not be rewarded or recognized. The killing became anonymous and lacked honor, grace, and audacity. The holder of the position of honor, the "spear point", would now become a useless death.

The use of muskets has been documented as early as 1543 in Japan; the guns were most probably brought as trade by the Chinese, the Portuguese, and later, the English and Dutch.

The Tanegashima musket, named for Tanegashima island, off Kyushu, is famous for guns. Mendez Pinto, a Portuguese voyager on his way to China, landed there in 1543 and introduced firearms to Japan. The name of the island came to mean "firearms" to the Japanese. From 1560, firearms were used in large battles in Japan.

In 1549, the famous Oda Nobunaga ordered 500 guns to be made for his armies. According to one estimate in 16th century Japan, an archer could fire 15 arrows in the time a gunner would take to load, charge, and shoot a firearm.

Regardless, at the Battle of Nagashino in 1575, three thousand gunners helped win the battle, firing by volleys of a thousand shots at a time.

The musket, followed by the rifle, and later the handgun, not only became the new martial weapon, but replaced the *wakazashi* and *katana* swords in many cases. The Japanese under the Tokugawa shogunate would close Japan to outside influences, and under the reign of the Tokugawa shoguns, the firearm would be shunned in favor of the sword again.

It makes sense to examine the modern Glock, Sig Sauer, Beretta, and other pistols in the context of martial art and martial science. The student should not think that a gun is not a "traditional" or martial weapon; the samurai of medieval Japan did not consider the musket to be unmanly or cowardly, and the most famous warlords in the history of Japan used them liberally. The firearm could be a conceptual extension of the two-handed sword.

Takeda Shingen, is said to have been invincible without relying on guns, because he studied Sun Tzu's *The Art of War*. This master work gave him the idea for his battle standard "*Fūrinkazan*" (風林火山), meaning "wind, forest, fire and mountain", taken to mean "fast as the wind, silent as a forest, ferocious as fire and immovable as a mountain".

William Scott Wilson personally told me of a popular version of the death of Shingen. During the siege of a castle, Shingen was entranced by the sound of a bamboo flute being played in the castle. Shingen had a chair set up so he could listen to the flautist. A lone sniper focused on the chair, and fired a single round, wounding Shingen, who eventually died, changing the course of Japanese history. The man that shunned the musket was killed by a single bullet, fired by a lone, anonymous sniper.

Iyeyasu himself was said to have believed that Shingen was to be the next *Shogun* of Japan. Upon Shingen's death, Uesugi Kenshin reportedly cried at the loss of one of his strongest and most deeply respected rivals.

The clan that would have had a thousand-year reign was soon ended. The forces of Tokugawa Ieyasu and Oda Nobunaga defeated the Takeda in the Battle of Nagashino. Oda Nobunaga's infantry, armed with Tanegashima muskets, destroyed the Takeda cavalry. Ieyasu then defeated the Takeda led by Takeda Katsuyori in the battle of Temmokuzan. Katsuyori committed *seppuku* after the battle, and the Takeda clan never recovered.

This lone sniper scene is poignantly depicted in the film *Kagemusha*, by director Akira Kurosawa.

Climb Mount Fuji,

O snail,

but slowly, slowly.

Kobayashi Issa
小林一茶

Go Rin No Sho:
The Book Of
Five Rings

Shimmen Miyamoto
Musashi Masana
宮本武蔵

Musashi is famous for his two-sword style (*Nitōjutsu*) which is the use of a *katana* (or *daitō*) and *wakizashi* (or *shōtō*) at the same time for fighting multiple opponents.

A modern warrior may consider carrying a main battle pistol and a backup, in the same way. Soldiers transition from the battle rifle to the handgun, and police officers carry a carbine or shotgun in the car, while carrying a pistol on the belt. But is this really the same?

Musashi eschewed the showy styles, and was blunt in his analysis that that excessive technical flourishes are useless, and pushed the principle that all technique is simply a method of defeating one's opponent.

Musashi's work is a compilation of his teachings to his private students and his students in his *dojo*, and should be taken as such. The term *"two swords, one spirit"* is ascribed to Musashi, but the concept of becoming one with the sword is also ascribed to him, as is the concept of becoming nothing.

In Yoshikawa's epic *Musashi*, Gudō the priest tells Musashi he has "not one thing" to offer him. Later, Gudō draws a circle around Musashi in the dirt. The circle is the symbol of the universe. When Musashi draws his sword, the circle is unchanged, but the shadow he casts makes the symbol for "o", the universe. When he draws his second sword, the circle still does not change. Two swords are as one.

In the world of firearms, transitioning from the long gun to the handgun should be seamless and natural, dropping the rifle and allowing the sling to take it away, while drawing the pistol. The fight continues, and nothing changes. The practitioner gets on target and fires with no thought of the difference between the handgun and the rifle. The change in sight radius does not change the universe.

A person skilled in the use of the pistol should be able to pick up any pistol and use it, regardless of the make or caliber. The debate of the Glock versus the 191 or the .40 versus the .45 is useless. A person skilled in billiards can shoot pool with a broom stick.

Musashi fought Sasaki Kojiro (Ganryu) using a wooden sword carved from a discarded oar, in his most famous battle, on the island of Funashima, on the straits of Shimonoseki. Does the caliber then really matter so very much, if the aim is true? Ganryu found out the hard way; Musashi killed him with one blow.

Musashi was also known as "*Niten*", his artistic name. Musashi, the fierce and fearless swordsman, was also *Niten*, the calligrapher and painter. The gentle side of Musashi was as gentle as the fierce side was fierce.

The town of Miyamoto in Mimasaka was a tough and dangerous place after the battle of Sekighara. Young men were out of work, and *ronin* did what they could for money. Our hero was tempered in the forge of adversity and poverty.

Musashi's life ended with his becoming an ascetic and his ascent to Mount Iwato. The sixty-two year old *zazen* master, painter, calligrapher, sculptor, and sword saint died in 1645. Before his passing, Musashi gave us his great work, *Go Rin No Sho*.

The Book of Earth discusses martial arts, leadership, and training. Training is described as building a house. This metaphor has been used many times to describe shooting, as in the fundamentals (stance, breath control, sight alignment, trigger squeeze, follow-though) are akin to the foundation.

Musashi stated that it is a rare person who follows the way of the martial arts. His book mentions that these skills may be useful in the world, that these skills are useful in all things. A person who carries a gun daily, who is ready to defend both himself and others, is a warrior of the highest order. When the lawful carrying of a firearm allows a citizen to defend others against mass murder, robbery, and terrorism, in a public place, the common man can be a hero.

The Book of Water describes Musashi's style, *Ni-ten ichi-ryu*, or "Two Heavens, One Style". "Two guns, one cop" can certainly describe the patrolman who has both an AR-15 and a Glock Pistol. Both are useful; both are useless. The shooter makes the difference.

Musashi advises to make the mind like water. Water takes the shape of its container. The modern fighter must understand the relationship of himself to his surroundings, to make use of cover and concealment.

Musashi also advised that the warrior temper himself with a thousand days of practice, and refine himself with ten thousand days of training. It is no coincidence that the modern firearms instructors mention that muscle memory takes one thousand repetitions, minimum.

The Book of Fire refers to the heat of battle, and may be somewhat similar to the code system used by the Jeff Cooper crowd. Jeff Cooper was a Marine Lieutenant Colonel who served in both

World War II and the Korean War. Cooper was well known as a gun writer.

Cooper used color codes to describe levels of combat readiness. These levels represent awareness and the ability to deal with threats; the codes range from Condition White, where one is totally oblivious to surroundings, to Condition Red, where one is fighting for life.

The Book of Wind discusses what Musashi considers to be the failings of various sword fighting schools. Many "gun gurus" show themselves to be inflexible when it comes to handgun choice and act as if the Colt M1911 is the only useable pistol and the .45 ACP is the only useable round.

Again, Musashi would cast off these problems as if casting off an old cloak, and attack, with little thought to the caliber and maker, only considering the shot, and making the shot perfect.

The Book of the Void is a commentary on Musashi's hard won Zen training and meditations on consciousness and the correct mindset. The warrior must be ready at all times, and become one with his equipment. The final thought in this book is "the mind is emptiness". Nothing must interfere with this.

Musashi is said to have made the acquaintance of Hon'ami Koetsu, an aesthetic, during the Kyoto Renaissance. The succession of Lord Oda Nobunaga, Lord Toyotomi Hideyoshi, and Shogun Tokugawa Iyeyasu heralded a period of creativity in the areas of poetry, calligraphy, painting, sculpture, *Cha-no-yu*, *Noh* acting, and pottery.

Today we are undergoing a similar renaissance in the areas of metallurgy, polymer technology, proxemics, man-machine interaction (MMI), and ergonomics.

The names Glock, Colt, Sig Sauer, Smith and Wesson, Ruger, Kimber, STI, Springfield Armory, Norinco, Les Baer, and Para-Ordinance, are making great strides, in the same way as the swords from Mino province (*Gokaden*) became known for sharpness and creativity. The *Sōshū* School, *Yamato* School, *Bizen* School, *Yamashiro* School, and the *Mino* School, were the greatest of their day.

Gorō Nyūdō Masamune was Japan's John Moses Browning; a genius who was Japan's greatest swordsmith. Muramasa Sengo, who came later, was Japan's Gaston Glock. The school of sword-making at Ise province became known for swords, as Austria became known for pistols after Glock.

Musashi's last work was *The Way of Self-Reliance*; the final thought in this work is "never depart from the way of the martial arts".

Hagakure:
The Book Of The
Samurai

·

Yamamoto Tsunetomo
山本常朝

The book *Hagakure* condenses Yamamoto Tsunetomo's views on *bushido*, the code of the samurai. *Bushido* is made up of three words, Bu (武) meaning "martial", Shi (士) meaning "gentleman", and Do (道) meaning "the way", so *Bushido* may mean "the way of the warrior-student". This translation is mine, from the original Japanese. The Kanji on the first page of this book is the word written out.

Hagakure is sometimes said to purport that bushido is really the "way of dying" or "living as though one was already dead", and that a warrior must be willing to die at any moment in order to truly serve his lord.

A modern police officer, soldier, or firearms enthusiast is more interested in living than were the samurai of medieval Japan.

Samurai (侍) meant "to serve", and the greatest service was to give one's life in battle for the glory of his lord. What more was there to give? The only thing that truly belonged to a *samurai* was his honor. Tsunetomo's saying "I have found the way of the warrior is death" was a manifestation of the sacrifice that *bushido* demanded.

It is clear that the modern Western person

cannot and will not meet the standards common to the Eastern warrior-poets who were contemporaries of Tsunetomo's in 1716. The Westerner sells his life dear and considers self-defense more important than self-sacrifice.

History tells us that Tsunetomo desired to commit *seppuku* (a more acceptable term than the baser *hara-kiri,* meaning "belly-cutting"), on the death of his master Nabeshima Mitsushige, but that honor had been denied by the policy of the Togugawa shogunate.

Tsunetomo believed that the pinnacle of the samurai's life was death. A direct death was preferable, but an honorable suicide was also desirable. To act as a second (*kaishaku*) was not desirable; it was considered ill-omened by samurai to be requested as *kaishaku*. The reason for this is that one gains no fame even if the job is well done.

Further, if one should blunder, it becomes a lifetime disgrace. Refusing to act as second was also dishonorable. In the 1600's, there were times when the head flew off. It was said that it was best to cut leaving a little skin remaining so that it did not fly off in the direction of the official witnesses.

Negligence was considered to be an ultimate evil or malfeasance. Tsunetomo stated "we all want to live", but at the same time, also noted that "the way of the samurai is found in death." Going out to meet death in a manly way was the ultimate expression of honor, duty, and service.

A modern Westerner must also keep in mind that holstering a handgun may mean that the duty to use the gun to defend innocents or family members may present itself, and the duty to act and perform in a way that is judicious, brave, and self-sacrificing, may present itself any day, in a shopping mall, in a restaurant, or in a bank.

The act of carrying a gun may place you in a position that if a bank robber were to discover your firearm, you may be killed on the spot. "Laying low" and waiting for the police may cause your death. Action is preferable to reaction.

The Life-Giving Sword: Secret Teachings From The House Of The Shogun

.

Yagyu Munenori
柳生宗矩

When Miyamoto Musashi was still learning the sword, already accomplished was Lord Yagyū Tajima no kami Munenori, the founder of the Edo school of Yagyū Shinkage-ryū, which he learned from his father Yagyū Sekishusai Muneyoshi.

Munenori and Sekishusai were both active during Musashi's life, but both were much superior in rank and skill at the time Musashi was learning. It may be that both Munenori and Sekishusai were teachers to Musashi.

The Yagyū were tutors to the Tokugawa Shogunate. This made the Yagyū School powerful and influential. Munenori served Tokugawa Ieyasu personally as tutor, and later was an instructor to Ieyasu's son Hidetada, teaching techniques learned from Kamiizumi Nobutsuna.

Because Musashi desired the position, and was unsuccessful, Yagyū Munenori was sometimes referred to as Musashi's "great rival", but both men would have considered jealousy to be a weakness to be avoided.

The concept of the "life-giving sword" (*Katsujinken*) is easily converted to the concept of the "life-giving gun". The pro-gun lobby celebrates the use of personal firearms for self-defense and defense of others.

A universal truth is that legally-owned fire-arms are used in more legitimate cases of heroic self-defense and defense of others, than illegally-owned firearms are used in crimes.

The concept of no-sword, or not being cut by an opponent's sword while yourself being unarmed, may be seen by the Westerner as bringing a knife to a gunfight. Toyogoro managed to defeat Yagyū Muneyoshi three times in a row. It is also said that Toyogoro was a master of the "no-sword" style of *bujutsu*, possibly the reason he defeated Muneyoshi. Although no-sword is undoubtedly powerful, I always advocate being armed with a full-size battle pistol, and stout folding knife, and a backup gun.

Munenori learned from Takuan Sōhō, a principal teacher to Musashi, to cast away all attachment, become enlightened, and seek the no-mind. Throughout the *Life-Giving Sword*, the influence of Takuan Sōhō, and especially his *Fudochi Shinmyo Roku*, is evident. Munenori's work is in part an examination of Takuan Sōhō's Zen thoughts from the standpoint of a swordsman. This is all but impossible for a Westerner to comprehend.

The Westerner must be concerned with criminal prosecution, civil liability, injury, death, and persecution. The Westerner is loath to use his handgun. Lord Yagyū states that "weapons are instruments of ill omen. The way of Heaven finds them repugnant. The way of Heaven is to use them only when necessary." This has remained unchanged in the last four hundred years.

The Unfettered Mind: Writings From A Zen Master To A Master Swordsman

.

Takuan Soho
沢庵宗彭

Takuan Sōhō, a Zen Buddhist monk, poet, calligrapher, strategist, philosopher, painter, gardener, and tea master, influenced both Musashi and Munenori, and in doing so, might just have been the greatest influence on martial thought of any man in Japan's history.

The Unfettered Mind, is a writing to Lord Yagyū Munenori. Takuan was convinced that the sword must be an extension of the Samurai's spirit, just as a handgun must be an extension of the shooter's hand. If a shooter points with his index finger, point-shooting states that the bullet will go there; the harder a shooter stares at the point of impact, the more likely the bullet will go to that point.

This is an amazing concept. Since the pistol was large, heavy, and ungainly at the time, this concept would have astounded these swordsmen. Superhuman speed and accuracy was available with the arrow at the time, but this concept was as of yet unavailable with the firearm.

Gudō Toshoku was a *Rinzai* Zen monk from the early Tokugawa period; he wrote *"I laugh at my ten year pilgrimage, wilted robe, tattered hat, knocking at Zen gates. In reality, the Buddha's law is simple: eat your rice, drink your tea, wear your clothes."*

Gudō left no book of writings, while Takuan Sōhō left six known volumes. The wisdom of the Abbott Gudō is lost, but that of Takuan Sōhō is available to us.

Not only did Takuan Sōhō advise Yagyū Munenori, but he also advised Ono Tadaaki, of the Itto School of swordsmanship; together these two schools were tutors to the Tokugawa Shoguns, the most famous and important in Japanese history. This renaissance flourished and nurtured martial science like no time period before or since.

Yagorō Itto Ittōsai Kagehisa's style evolved from the Tomita and Chujo-ryu styles of his master, Kanemaki Jisai. Among the many successors that Ittōsai trained, one was his successor, Ono Tadaaki, who was also advised by Takuan Sōhō.

This litany of martial men, Itto Ittōsai, Kanemaki Jisai, Takuan Sōhō, Yagyū Munenori, Ono Tadaaki, and Miyamoto Musashi, formed a mélange of ideas that were so revolutionary, that it would have been overwhelming to even conceive of the exchange or information between Takuan Sōhō and those he advised. If the six should get together (there is no evidence they ever did), the air would have been supercharged with the spirit of the four giants of the Zen martial world.

There is no parallel that can be drawn to modern ideas and weaponry. If Gaston Glock, Bill Ruger, Uzi Galil, Mikhail Kalashnikov, and John Moses Browning got together (an impossibility), the likelihood is that they would have bored each other.

Takuan stated that nothing is dearer to us than life, but that life is of small account compared to right-mindedness. There is nothing more esteemed than right-mindedness. This concept is as valid today as it was four centuries ago.

The Art
Of War

·

Sun Tzu
孫武

Sun Tzu's *Art of War* has grown in popularity in Western society, and his work has continued to influence both Asian and Western culture and politics. It is commonly known that the Asian businessman keeps *The Art of War* on his desk.

There are many books on strategy, and there are books on tactics. Tactics and strategy are different.

The Art of War is one of the oldest and most important books on military strategy in the world. It has had an influence on Eastern military thinking, business tactics, and beyond. *The Art of War* has been much more influential than Carl Philipp Gottfried von Clausewitz' *On War (Vom Kriege)* which was unfinished at his death. *On War* is seen as the West's premier work on the philosophy of war, and an answer to the East's *The Art of War*. The gun culture has no such treatise.

von Clausewitz stated that "strategy" belongs primarily to the realm of art, while "tactics" belongs primarily to the realm of science. Michael Handel wrote *Masters of War: Classical Strategic Thought,* which was largely comparison of Clausewitz's *On War* with Sun Tzu's *The Art of War.* It is not unusual to think that these two minds, one Eastern, one Western, would be compared and contrasted.

This analysis of the classical works by von Clausewitz, Sun Tzu, Mao Tse-tung, Jomini, and Machiavelli, is worth reading. I would recommend a glass of port and a good pipe as companions.

Many "gun gurus" espouse von Clausewitz, and the nature of war as being universal. There is some merit to this. Many "gun gurus" served in the military in forward units and saw combat.

The United States Army, through the Command and General Staff College, has directed all units to maintain a copy of *The Art of War*. *The Art of War* is listed on the Marine Corps Professional Reading Program (Commandant's Reading List). It is recommended reading for all United States Military Intelligence personnel and is required reading for all CIA officers. The book is also required reading for many lawyers, businessmen, and sports coaches.

When I chant,

both Buddha and self

cease to exist.

Namu amida butsu,

Namu amida butsu.

Ippen Shonin
一遍上人

One Man's Dream:
The Polymer Pistol.
Twenty-Five Years
of the
Glock 17

.

Gaston Glock

When discussing firearms, one must never forget the saga of Gaston Glock. Glock may have never read the *Go Rin No Sho*. I have no way of knowing if he did or not; yet Glock was the personification of the old Zen adage *"do not seek to change the course of the river: steer the boat!"*

There are many wonderful representations of the pistol. John Moses Browning's M1911 has been produced by such powerhouses as Colt, Sig Sauer, Smith and Wesson, Ruger, Remington, Kimber, STI, Springfield Armory, Norinco, Les Baer, and others. They were also made by such diverse companies as Singer Sewing Machine, Union Switch & Signal, and Rockola Juke Box.

Most pistols made today are adaptations from Browning's designs. Glock had never designed a gun, and began from the beginning, ignoring the designs of John Browning. The Zen *koan "what is the sound of one hand clapping?"* was answered when Glock's new design took shape. Like the rending of a cloud, the gun world changed, never to be the same.

Men have been killing each other for thousands of years. Arrows, spears, fists, feet, maces, staffs, knives, and agricultural tools of every shape and type have been used to take up arms against tyrants, defend the weak, uphold the law, and unite countries against foreign invaders.

When gunpowder was invented, the martial world changed. Canon, explosives, war rockets, muskets, and fireworks changed the way men warred.

It is hard to pinpoint the decade that the ancient straight swords from the *Asuka* and *Nara* periods gave way to the curved swords of the *Heian* period, and we do not know the name of the swordsmith who decided to change the way swords were made.

It is hard to pinpoint the decade the Chinese discovered gunpowder, or just when the matchlock musquette was made. Time has erased the name of the man who formed this first long gun from heat and metal.

Gaston Glock brought his gun to the market in 1986. We know the year. This man changed the course of warfare. We know his name. Will the name John Moses Browning be remembered? Will the name of Gaston Glock, the one man who dared to be different from Browning be remembered? Does the mountain remember the name of Musashi, who lived on the mountain?

Looking Toward
The Future,
Respecting The Past

.

100 Years of the American
M1911 .45 ACP

.

One Thousand Years
of Japanese Swordsmanship

It is the year 2011. This is the observance of 100 years of the M1911 .45 ACP. It is particularly fitting that the pistol was developed in response to Asians.

The M1911 is a single-action, semi-automatic, magazine-fed, and recoil-operated handgun chambered for the .45 ACP cartridge.

John Moses Browning designed the firearm which was the side arm for the United States military from 1911 to 1985, and is still carried by some U.S. forces and police officers. It was widely used in World War I, World War II, the Korean War, and the Vietnam War. Millions of these models were produced by dozens of companies all over the world.

US forces encountered by fierce fighting from Moro guerrillas during the Philippine-American War (Moro Rebellion) The word *Moro* was a term for Muslims who lived in the southern Philippines, an area that includes Mindanao. The Moro would wrap themselves in rope and take certain drugs when fighting. The Colt M1892 revolver, in .38 LC, was inadequate in terms of stopping power.

The Moro were fierce and brave and in many cases, had nothing but long knives, The *Keris* or *Kris*, the *Barong* or the Bolo Machete, but the Army was unsettled. The M1873 single-action revolver in .45 Colt caliber, was used briefly, and the heavier bullet was more satisfactory.

Chief of Ordnance, General William Crozier, authorized further testing for a new service pistol in .45 caliber, which would become the M 1911; the rest was history. Only Colt and Savage were finalists, and in the end, the Savage design was found wanting.

Bujutsu train their students in martial methods to use *Katana* swords against classic Japanese steel weapons, while teaching the students tactics offered by the individual school, just as modern training centers Gunsite, LFI, and Thunder Ranch do. In the same way certain *ryu* were said to be the best, and success was sometimes determined by the possession of a certificate from the Itto or Yagyū schools, so the modern student retains bragging rights for attending these shooting schools.

Iaido is a martial art that trains students in the motions associated with drawing a sword, cutting an opponent, cleaning the blood from the blade, and then replacing the sword in the scabbard in smooth, stylized movements. One of the greatest of the teachers of this art was Katayama

Hōki-no-kami. Hisayasu. Legend has it that Itto Ittōsai could unconsciously and without thinking draw his sword and cut down an opponent in one lightning-fast stroke; drawing a gun from a holster is similar in concept.

Itto Ittōsai developed "*Hosshato*" when engaging multiple enemies. The shooting schools teach to engage multiple attackers. Musashi developed the pine-needle return strike, a fast stroke that uses a forward and return that looks like a pine needle, joined at the end ">". This sounds conspicuously like a "double-tap".

The greatest lesson taught, and the way I wish to end this discourse, is with a story about Tsukahara Bokuden. It is possible that Bokuden might have been influenced by Sun Tzu's quote, *"one hundred victories in one hundred battles is not the most skillful. Seizing the enemy without fighting is the most skillful."* Takeda Shingen certainly studied this work; he said to have become invincible in all battles without relying on guns, because he studied *The Art of War*.

It is related that Bokuden was challenged by an unknown *ronin*. Bokuden told the *ronin* that he studied the style of "no-sword." The *ronin* rudely challenged Bokuden to fight him "without a sword".

Bokuden agreed to fight the *ronin* without his sword, but insisted they row out to a nearby island to avoid disturbing others.

When the *ronin* leapt from the boat to the sand and drew his sword, Bokuden pushed the boat back out, leaving him stranded on the island. Bokuden explained, "*This is my no-sword school.*"

The only way to win a gunfight completely is to not be involved in a gunfight. This is my "no-gun school". This is all that I have to teach.

When I am at work, the mountain looks at me.

When I am at rest, I look at the mountain.

Though it seems the same, it is not the same,

For work is inferior to leisure.

Tsai Wen
蔡文

Adding the Firearm
to the Japanese Vocabulary

•

The Firearm as a Martial
Arts Weapon

Kobudo is a Japanese term that can be translated as "old martial way." It was formerly known as *Kobujutsu ("old martial art")*. With the advent of martial arts generally becoming practiced for reasons other than that of practicality, it is now more commonly known as *Kobudo*. The suffix *jutsu* is a stronger version than the suffix *do*.

Kenjutsu means "the method, or technique, of the sword." This is opposed to *Kendo*, which means "the way of the sword". So *Kendo* is akin to sword-study, while *Kenjutsu* is the proactive of sword techniques. This would be true with *Iaijutsu* and *Iaido* (the Japanese martial art associated with the smooth, controlled movements of drawing the sword from its scabbard) as well.

The martial art of wielding the *Jō* (four foot staff) is called *Jōjutsu* or *Jōdō*. The martial art of wielding the *Bō* (three foot staff) is called *Bō-jutsu* or *Bōdō*.

The *Kusarigama* ("chain-sickle" or "chain-ball-sickle") is a traditional weapon which consists of a *Kama* (the Japanese sickle) on a metal chain (*Kusari*) with a heavy iron weight (*Fundo*) at the end. The martial art of fighting with the *Kusarigama* is called *Kusarigamajutsu*.

This is the same with the hand-to-hand arts of *Jujutsu* (as opposed to *Judō*); *Jujutsu* leads to obtaining the lifestyle of *Judō. Aikijutsu* leads to obtaining the lifestyle of *Aikido*); other studies include *Kyūdō* (archery, or "way of the bow") using a *Yumi*, or six foot bow; the martial art of wielding the *Naginata* (five to seven foot spear) is known as *Naginatajutsu*.

Budō is a Japanese term describing martial arts. In English, it is used almost exclusively in reference to Japanese martial arts. *Budō* is a compound of the root *bu*, meaning war or martial; and *dō*, meaning path or way. *Bujutsu*, meaning martial or military art or science, is the practical application of techniques of *Budō* to battlefield situations. *Budō* has a more philosophical emphasis, a philosophical path.

Bushi is a name for *Samurai* warrior class used in the term *Bushidō in* the 13th to 16th centuries. The foremost research into *Bushidō* was conducted by William Scott Wilson in his 1982 text *Ideals of the Samurai: Writings of Japanese Warriors*. Wilson's book examined the most important Japanese writings in the 8th century: the Kojiki (712 AD), Shoku Nihongi (797 AD), the Kokin Wakashū (10th century), Konjaku Monogatari (1106) and the Heike Monogatari (1371), as well as the Chinese Classics (the Analects, the Great Learning, the Doctrine of the Mean, and the Mencius (500 BC).

The ten virtues of the *Bushidō* code:

Rectitude (義, *gi*)
Courage (勇, *yū*)
Benevolence (仁, *jin*)
Respect (礼, *rei*)
Honesty (誠, *makoto*)
Honor (名誉, *meiyo*)
Loyalty (忠義, *chūgi*)
Filial piety (孝, *kō*)
Wisdom (智, *chi*)
Care for the aged (悌, *tei*)

These virtues can be traced back to the Buddhist "Noble Eightfold Path" (*Hasshōdō*) that can be regarded as a progressive list of virtues.

- Right View - Realizing the Four Noble Truths (*samyag-dṛṣṭi, sammā-diṭṭhi*).

- Right Intention - Commitment to mental and ethical growth in moderation (*samyak-saṃkalpa, sammā-saṅkappa*).

- Right Speech - One speaks in a non-hurtful, not exaggerated, truthful way (*samyag-vāc, sammā-vācā*).

- Right Action - Wholesome action, avoiding action that would do harm (*samyak-karmānta, sammā-kammanta*).

- Right Livelihood - One's job does not harm in any way oneself or others; directly or indirectly (*samyag-ājīva, sammā-ājīva*).

- Right Effort - One makes an effort to improve (*samyag-vyāyāma, sammā-vāyāma*).

- Right Mindfulness - Mental ability to see things for what they are with clear consciousness (*samyak-smṛti, sammā-sati*).

- Right Concentration - Wholesome "one-pointedness" of mind (*samyak-samādhi, sammā-samādhi*).

The Four Noble Truths are an important principle in Buddhism, classically taught by the Buddha in the *Dharmacakra Pravartana Sūtra*. Prince Siddhārtha Gautama, (The Buddha) described them as the way leading to The Noble Eightfold Path. The Four Noble Truths are:

- Suffering does exist.

- Suffering arises from attachment to desires.

- Suffering ceases when attachment to desire ceases.

- Freedom from suffering is possible by practicing the Eightfold Path.

This could be compared and contrasted to the four classical Western "cardinal virtues" from Greek:

Temperance: σωφροσύνη (*sōphrosynē*)
Prudence: φρόνησις (*phronēsis*)
Fortitude: ανδρεία (*andreia*)
Justice: δικαιοσύνη (*dikaiosynē*)

"If a man does not investigate into the matter of Bushidō daily, it will be difficult for him to die a brave and manly death. Thus, it is essential to engrave this business of the warrior into one's mind well."

Kato Kiyomasa

From "a handbook addressed to all samurai, regardless of rank" reprinted in *Ideals of the Samurai: Writings of Japanese Warriors*
By William Scott Wilson

"It is shameful for any man to die without having risked his life in battle, regardless of rank, and that Bushidō is in being crazy to die. Fifty or more could not kill one such a man."

Nabeshima Naoshige
From Lord Nabeshima's Wall Inscriptions
Reprinted in *Ideals of the Samurai: Writings of Japanese Warriors*
By William Scott Wilson

Given that we can now discuss the suffixes – jutsu and –do, it is important to examine the "Japanization" of English words. The Japanese word for "knife" is "*Hōchō*", but many Japanese now use "*naifu*". Given this, there may be several new terms to come from this examination: Until modern times, firearms were colloquially known in Japan as "*Tanegashima*", so *Tanegashimadō,* would be obtaining the lifestyle of the *Tanegashima* or "guncraft", whereas *Tanegashimajutsu* would be the martial art of firing a *Tanegashima* gun.

Hōjutsu was a school or style of musketry that dealt with stylized versions of firing the matchlock musket or matchlock hand-cannon. The *Seki-Ryū* school of *Hōjutsu* was founded by Seki Hachizaemon in 1617. The immense *bassanjū* cannon required the shooter to aim, fire, and absorb tremendous recoil, and do so in a stylized way; being knocked down by the blow-back of such an arm would have been shameful.

While it is commonly held that the French invented the bayonet in Bayonne around 1700, there is anecdotal evidence of bayonet use in the Japans in the 1600's. European bayonet techniques were brought to Japan during the Meiji era in the mid 1800's. *Jūsō-Jutsu,* using the bayonet mounted musket as a spear, was introduced in this period as well.

Documented use of the bayonet is noted in the Satsuma rebellion of 1877, a revolt of Satsuma *Samurai* against Meiji government soldiers from January 29 to September 24, 1877, nine years into the Meiji Era. During the Meiji period, Japanese bayonet fighting techniques were practiced as *Jūken-jitsu*.

Modern *Jūkendō* is the style or school of bayonet fighting. The chest, shoulder, left arm, left shoulder, left hand, and throat are the primary targets attacked by practitioners using the long musket with a bayonet attached; in practice sessions, a *Mokujū* or wooden practice musket with a rubber cap is used.

Jūkendō is practiced in Japan today, as well as *Tankendō*, using the bayonet detached from the long arm. Special padding is worn which is thicker at the abdomen and throat than *Kendō* padding. The All-Japan Jūkendō Federation (AJJF) exists today, and is made up of over forty organizations of *Jūkendō* practitioners. *Dan* ranks in *Jūkendō* are issued by prefectural and regional federations, and teaching certificates at eighth *dan* and higher are issued by AJJF. Referee certificates are also issued this way.

As of 2009, there were 47,000 registered members of the All-Japan Jūkendō Federation; according to the *Nippon Budokan*, there are an estimated half-million practitioners of *Jūkendō* in the world today, some of whom compete in national competitions and tournaments.

But what of modern firearms? there has been talk for over two decades of a black-belt or *dan* ranking in shooting, and many have explained their interest in firearms in a martial context. The idea of becoming one with the gun, in the same way an archer became one with the *yumi* (bow), in order to mentally send the projectile to the heart of the target, has its roots in ten-thousand-year-old *Kyūdō* archery techniques.

I therefore propose the adoption of the following terms by the American martial arts community: *Gūndō,* obtaining the lifestyle of guncraft; *Gūnjutsu,* The martial art of firing a gun; *Firamudō,* obtaining the lifestyle of a firearm expert; *Firamujutsu,* The martial art of firing a firearm; *Raifudō,* obtaining the lifestyle of a sniper; *Raifujutsu,* The martial art of firing a rifle; *Shutudō,* obtaining the lifestyle of a shootist, and *Shutujutsu,* The martial art of shooting.

One day, a *Kyōju Dairi*, a teaching certificate of the type earned in various Japanese *koryū*, or traditional martial arts, may be earned in these aforementioned arts.

One must realize that the *Samurai* believed that *katana* and even *yumi* had a spirit and a soul. While no one would think of a mass-produced Heckler and Koch MP5 or a Beretta M92 could be infused with a "soul" at the factory, one must remember the *Zen koan* "Joshu's Dog", a riddle whereby a scholar asks if a dog has a soul:

A monk asked Joshu, a Chinese *Zen* master: "has a dog Buddha-nature or not?" Joshu answered: "*Mu*", meaning there is no answer. There is never really an answer to a *Zen* riddle, but the following was offered:

> *Has a dog Buddha-nature?*
> *This is the most serious question of all.*
> *If you say yes or no,*
> *You lose your own Buddha-nature.*

So using this lesson as a guide, there is no way to tell if *katana* and *yumi* had a spirit or a soul, but under the exactly correct conditions, the use of the gun might just in fact, polish the soul of the user.

This offers us something to think about.

"Hereafter, the guns will be the most important arms. Therefore decrease the number of spears per unit, and have your most capable men carry guns."

Takeda Shingen (1567)
Instructions to his officers
Quoted in *Giving Up the Gun: Japan's Reversion to the Sword*
By Noel Perrin

"You should not have any special fondness for a particular weapon, or anything else, for that matter. Too much is the same as not enough. Without imitating anyone else, you should have as much weaponry as suits you."

Miyamoto Musashi

References:

Budo: Martial Ways of Japan by Nippon Budokan, edited by Alexander Bennett. Tokyo, Japan: Nippon Budokan (2009).

Collapse of the Tokugawa Bakufu, 1862–1868, by Conrad Totman. Honolulu: University of Hawaii Press. (1980).

Giving up the Gun, Japan's reversion to the Sword, 1543–1879, by Noel Perrin. Boston: David R. Godine. (1979).

Go Rin No Sho, by Miyamoto Musashi. (translation by William Scott Wilson). New York: Kodansha America, Inc. (2002)

Hagakure, by Yamamoto Tsunetomo. (translation by William Scott Wilson). New York: Kodansha America, Inc. (2002).

Ideals of the Samurai: Writings of Japanese Warriors, by William Scott Wilson. New York: Kodansha America, Inc. (1982).

Masters of War: Classical Strategic Thought by Michael Handel. Portland, Oregon: Frank Cass Publishers. (2001).

Musashi by Eiji Yoshikawa. (translation by Charles S. Terry). New York: Kodansha America, Inc. (1995).

Samurai - The World of the Warrior by Stephen Turnbull. UK: Osprey Publishing (2006).

Taiko by Eiji Yoshikawa (translation by William Scott Wilson).New York: Kodansha America, Inc. (2001).

Tao Te Ching by Lao Tzu. (translation by William Scott Wilson). New York: Kodansha America, Inc. (2010).

Tanegashima: the arrival of Europe in Japan by Olof G. Lidin. Copenhaden, Denmark: Nordic Institute of Asian Studies. (2002).

The Art of War, by Sun Tzu. (translation by Lionel Giles). Lexington, KY: SoHo Books. (2003).

The Life-Giving Sword, by Yagyū Munenori. (translation by William Scott Wilson). New York: Kodansha America, Inc.(2003).

The Lone Samurai, by William Scott Wilson. New York: Kodansha America, Inc. (2004).

The political economy of merchant empires: State Power and World Trade, 1350–1750. Edited by James D. Tracy. New York: Cambridge University Press. (1992).

Tao Te Ching: An All-New Translation by Lao-Tzu and William Scott Wilson. New York: Kodansha America, Inc. (2010).

The Unfettered Mind, by Takuan Sōhō. (translation by William Scott Wilson). New York: Kodansha America, Inc. (2003).

A man's fate

is a man's fate,

and life is but an illusion;

a dream within a dream.

Guró Michael
Weissberg

Harvest moon,

Called at his house;

He was digging potatoes.

Yosa Buson
与謝蕪村

Pen and Ink on paper rendering: "*Musashi Being Taught by the Tengu Sōjōbō on Mt. Kuriyama*", by Grandmaster Bram Frank. Concept of "*Musashi Being Taught by the Tengu Sōjōbō on Mt. Kuriyama*" by author Michael W. Weissberg.

Author's notes on the *Tengu:*

Tengu are mystical creatures found in Japanese legends, art, *Nōh* theater, and literature. They are revered as *Shinto kami* (spirits). According to legend, the mountain *Tengu* Sōjōbō, the mythical king of the Tengu, taught swordsmanship to the famous swordsman Minamoto no Yoshitsune on Mt. Kuriyama, a Japanese holy mountain.

Another story tells of a girl with no skill who is possessed by a *Tengu.* Soon a young samurai arrives; the *Tengu* has appeared to him in a dream, and the possessed girl teaches him to be an expert swordsman.

In another legend, a boy is carried off by a *Tengu* and spends three years with the spirit. He comes home with a magic gun that never misses a shot.

Some rumors surrounding the *ninja* indicate that they were instructed by the *Tengu.*

Although there are no known legends or rumors about Miyamoto Musashi having been taught by *Tengu*, he was so skilled, that people in his time may have ascribed his ability to the *Tengu,* since they could not understand how a simple country *samurai* without a formal certificate of training could defeat so many famous warriors.

I envisioned Musashi defeating a member of the Obata school or the Yoshioka school, and two townsmen wondering aloud if this provincial swordsman could have been taught by *Tengu.* I then provided some sketches to Grandmaster Bram Frank, and asked him to render a pen and ink drawing or painting.

It is known that Musashi himself was often asked to leave a painting behind as a token, when he departed from visiting a lord, perhaps even leaving a painting for the *Shogun Tokugawa Iyeyasu* himself. Musashi was known to paint in simple but bold strokes, and greatly admired the Chinese painter Liang-K'ai.

Here, Bram has rendered the *Tengu* in bold, sure strokes, and shows Musashi learning from and being possessed by the *Tengu,* who envelops Musashi, and radiates from both Musashi's mind via his *ajna* or brow *chakra* (also known as the "third eye" or "inner eye" in Sanskrit) and his Japanese *hara,* or center, also known as the *manipura,* or navel *chakra* (also known as the "center of being", in Sanskrit, or in yoga philosophy, the seat of *Prana*).

I hope this collaborative effort by Grand-master Frank and me pleases the reader, and gives pause: what if the tengu were real? What if Musashi was possessed by *Tengu*? And what would Japan and the martial arts world have been like without *Tanegashima* firearms, or without Musashi?   Did the arrival of the firearm change everything, like the rending of a cloud, never to be the same again? What is the sound of one hand clapping?

NOTES

NOTES

NOTES

NOTES

NOTES

NOTES

"Before enlightenment, chop wood and carry water.

After enlightenment, chop wood and carry water."

Wu Li
吳歷

WHITE MOUNTAIN PUBLISHING CO.
MIAMI, FLORIDA
2011

www.ingramcontent.com/pod-product-compliance
Lightning Source LLC
Chambersburg PA
CBHW062050090426
42740CB00016B/3078

* 9 7 8 0 9 8 3 4 8 6 6 5 7 *